Alma Flor Ada

UNDER
— THE —
ROYAL
PALMS

A CHILDHOOD IN CUBA

ATHENEUM BOOKS FOR YOUNG READERS

Atheneum Books for Young Readers
An imprint of Simon & Schuster Children's Publishing Division
1230 Avenue of the Americas
New York, New York 10020

Book design by Nina Barnett
The text of this book is set in Baskerville Book.

0814 FFG
Printed in the United States of America
20

Library of Congress Cataloging-in-Publication Data
Under the royal palms : a childhood in Cuba / by Alma Flor Ada.

p. cm.
Summary: The author recalls her life and impressions growing up
in Cuba.
ISBN-13: 978-0-689-80631-5 (ISBN-10: 0-689-80631-0)
1. Ada, Alma Flor—Childhood and youth—Juvenile literature.
2. Authors, American—20th century—Biography—Juvenile literature.
3. Authors, Cuban—20th century—Biography—Juvenile literature.
4. Ada, Alma Flor—Homes and haunts—Cuba—Juvenile literature.
5. Cuban American women—Biography—Juvenile literature. 6. Cuba—
Social life and customs—Juvenile literature. 7. Family—Cuba—Juvenile
literature. [1. Ada, Alma Flor. 2. Authors, American. 3. Cuba—Social
life and customs. 4. Women—Biography.] I. Title.
PS3551.D22Z475   1998
813'.54—dc21
[B]
97-48887

GRATEFULLY:

To Quica,
who builds bridges out of sun beams.

To Jon Lanman,
who turns dreams into books.

To Rosalma,
grateful for your unending support
and for being who you are.

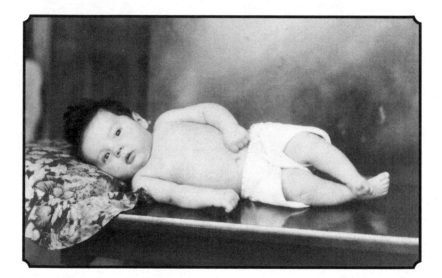

✦ ALMA FLOR ADA ✦

47 DAYS OLD

Contents

✦ WITH MY MOTHER AND FATHER ✦

Introduction

During my childhood I lived in Camagüey, the city where I was born, in the eastern part of Cuba, one of the many islands in the Caribbean Sea. The four larger islands in the Caribbean are called Greater Antilles. They include Hispaniola, the island shared by Haiti and the Dominican Republic; Puerto Rico; Jamaica; and Cuba. Of all these islands, Cuba, long and narrow, is the largest of all. It lies very close to the southern tip of Florida. Because Cuba is located at the entrance to the Gulf of Mexico, it is sometimes called "the Key to the Gulf." On account of its beauty, its fertile land, and its incomparable weather, never too humid nor too hot, it is also called "the Pearl of the Antilles."

When I was growing up, Camagüey was a quiet place. In Cuba we called it a city, but in a larger country it would have been called a town. Many of its streets were narrow and winding, and most were paved with stones. After a rain, the gray stones were slippery and dangerous for the horses that pulled the carts of the milkmen, the bakers, and the coal vendors. It always upset me deeply to see a horse slip and fall on the wet stones. Not many people had private cars. Most used public transportation: crowded buses or slow and noisy streetcars called *tranvías*. We also probably walked much more than most people in the United States today, to go to school or to work, to go shopping, or to visit relatives or friends in the afternoon, something we often did without giving them notice and a custom we all welcomed.

The majority of the houses had tile roofs, with gutters to gather the rainwater. The colonial houses in the center of town were spacious, usually built around a central courtyard, with large doors and windows that went from ceiling to floor and were protected by carved wooden railings.

It was a city of contrasts. Contrasts in the way people behaved, in their beliefs and in their practices. Although most people would have called Cuba a Catholic country, in reality there were people from many religious traditions. The African people who had been held in slavery used many Catholic symbols and images to continue practicing their own beliefs under the cover of Catholicism. A few people had become Protestants, following the preaching of various American missionaries: Episcopalian, Baptist, Methodist, Adventist. There have always been Jewish people in Spanish-speaking countries, and many more arrived in Cuba fleeing Europe during World War II. Chinese people had been lured to Cuba with the promise of free land. After long years of indentured work on the fields, their perseverance and hard work had allowed most of them to settle in the cities where they owned stores, restaurants, laundry services, or vegetable gardens. Although some of them adopted Christian beliefs, many retained their ancestral religious practices. And then there were the freethinkers, maybe the fewest in number, who believed that spirituality need not be expressed under any specific set of rules.

There was a small, economically powerful circle of landowners, cattle ranchers, or professionals who observed European customs and considered themselves more refined. They listened to classical music, went to fine art exhibitions, and longed for theater and ballet. They spoke with controlled voices that displayed their education.

And then there was a much greater number of working people, mostly strong, loud, and boisterous, filled with energy and life, whose education was very different from that provided by the schools—theirs was the education of home traditions and long-held beliefs.

The most striking contrasts for me were not the differences in education and beliefs. The largest, most significant contrast was that some had so much and others had very little. While for some life was easy, almost a paradise on this beautiful island, for others the struggle to stay alive was extremely demanding. Many, especially young children, did not survive.

Even when I was only a child, these contrasts confused and concerned me. Because Cuba was a very young republic—it had won its independence from Spain in 1889 and from the U.S. in 1902, less than forty years before I was born—I heard many stories of the struggle for independence, of the dreams that had inspired the struggle, and of the heroes who had led the way. And I looked around me to see if those ideals were indeed alive, only to be saddened when I realized that in most ways, they were not. In the countryside, the majestic royal palms, symbols of Cuban independence, towered above the surrounding trees. But beneath those palms I saw too much poverty and too much pain, and I knew that the realization of the dreams of justice and equality were still far away.

My own family was not among the more affluent, but the hard work of many family members who shared the same house kept us from suffering the needs of those who had so little. Yet this was a constant cause of concern and struggle within me. Although very early on I began to realize that real wealth did not lie in material things, my heart was still saddened by those who suffered so much just to survive.

I was born in an old house, *La Quinta Simoni,* a house built during colonial times for an Italian family. One of their daughters, Amalia Simoni, had been born in the house. She married a young lawyer, Ignacio Agramonte, who later wrote the first Constitution of the insurgents, and fought against the Spanish army to free Cuba from Spanish domination. It moved me to know that the house I loved, that was my own world, had been where Ignacio and Amalia had met, spent time together, and briefly lived after their marriage. Later, Ignacio was killed in battle, and his ashes were scattered because the Spanish government did not want his tomb to become a shrine. For me, the garden where he had strolled with Amalia, the porch where they had exchanged sweet words of love and shared their dreams for an independent Cuba, were indeed a shrine to their ideals.

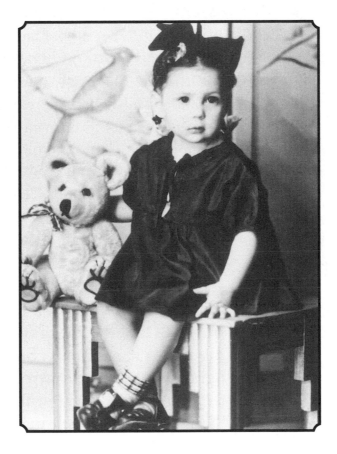

✦ ALMA FLOR ADA ✦

3 YEARS OLD

My beloved grandmother explained those ideals of freedom and equality to me every evening during the few years we shared. Later, after her death, the house became for us a shrine to her memory as well. In both this book and its companion volume, *Where the Flame Trees Bloom,* I have shared some of the feelings and memories of my childhood as well as some of the stories that were told to me. Sharing them is my own way of keeping these memories alive, and to continue to understand life. I have called this book *Under the Royal Palms* because the royal palm, standing majestic and alone, rising above the trees that surround it, is the symbol of an independent Cuba.

I hope that you will see my stories as an invitation for you to discover the many stories in your own life, and the meaning that they hold for you. ✦

✦ A ROYAL PALM TREE ✦

✦ LA QUINTA SIMONI ✦

THE BATS

Daily life in *La Quinta Simoni* started very early in the morning. The placid night fragances of jasmine and gardenias, which entered my bedroom from the garden, were quickly overtaken by the acrid but friendly smell of coffee brewing.

Before I was fully awake, my grandmother would often scoop me in her arms to take me to where they were milking the cows she still kept. Her neck smelled of fresh talcum, and her dress, invariably white, of lavender and sage.

When we returned to the house, everyone would be bustling about, getting ready to leave—my father to teach at the high school, my uncle Manolo to the radio station, my uncle Medardo to his office, my aunt Lolita to her classes, and my grandmother to the school she ran.

Before long the big house was all my mother's and mine. While she worked on her bookkeeping ledgers, I would spend hours playing outside, under the trees, just by myself.

Every afternoon, around four o'clock, I had to take a bath and get dressed "for the evening." I would set aside the boots I hated, with their hard insoles to support my flat feet, and put on my white shoes with a little strap on top and a buckle on the side. As my mother tied the bow at the back of my dress, I felt like a butterfly, daily forced to return to her chrysalis, and daily freed again.

The next thing to be done each afternoon was to gather *maravillas*. These simple wild flowers—red, orange, white, purple, or spotted—opened late in the day. It was as if, like me, they led two lives; one curled up and wrinkled in the heat of the day, one open and splendid in the late afternoon as the sun began to go down. They grew plentifully on an empty lot about half a block from the old *Quinta Simoni*. I would walk proudly down the sidewalk, glancing at my shoes, ready to gather as many flowers as I could.

On my return, my grandmother would be waiting for me on the front porch, sitting in a rocking chair, ready to praise the beauty of my simple offering. Then, we would both go on tiptoes, as if approaching an altar, to place the flowers on top of the piano, a ritual that pleased us both. We made garlands to wrap around the bust of José Martí, the Cuban poet and hero during the struggle for independence, and a doll wearing typical Mayan dress that someone had brought my grandmother from Guatemala. My grandmother would smile and say: "For Martí and *his niña de Guatemala*." I would smile, too, because the poem that Martí had written for a young girl in Guatemala, although very sad, was one of my favorites. And I loved that my grandmother had decided to unite, on top of her piano, the poet and the girl who had died loving him.

Once the ritual was finished, we would walk hand in hand out to the large front porch with its high masonry arches. She would sit in the rocking chair. I would sit on the steps a few feet away, listening to her sing verses set to music she herself had composed:

Quiero a la sombra de un ala
contar este cuento en flor
la niña de Guatemala
la que se murió de amor.

Under the shadow of a wing,
I will let this story blossom,
of a young Guatemalan girl,
who died of a broken heart.

The setting sun would turn the sky bright orange, and my grandmother would begin a new song:

Cultivo una rosa blanca
en junio como en enero,
para el amigo sincero
que me da su mano franca.
Y para el cruel, que me arranca
el corazón con que vivo,
cardos ni ortigas cultivo,
cultivo una rosa blanca.

I tend with care a white rose
both in January and in June
for the true friend
who offers a sincere hand.
And for the cruel one
who tears out my beating heart
I tend neither thistles nor thorns,
I tend with care a white rose.

And the night would fall around us, almost without notice, as it does in the tropics. Then the first of the bats would appear. They lived above the porch, between the ceiling and the roof. We never saw or heard them during the day. But at nightfall their squeaks began, like an orchestra tuning its instruments before a concert, and it was as if the ceiling came alive.

Occasionally, a little one would fall to the floor through a crack in the ceiling either pushed by a thoughtless adult or as a result of its own carelessness. Even though it was not ready to fly yet, by instinct the little bat would open its membranous wings, glide down, and land alive, although perhaps somewhat stunned. Sometimes an adult bat would come immediately to the rescue. Then the little one would cling to the adult's chest and enjoy a safe return home. But on occasions when no adult came, we had to decide whether to fetch the tall ladder and try to place the baby back in the nest, or keep it in a shoe box and feed it with my doll's bottle. Fortunately, this only happened once in a while.

Most nights, my grandmother and I would pretend to

✦ MY GRANDMOTHER LOLA ✦

DOLORES SALVADOR MÉNDEZ

count the bats as they left their nest to feed on the fruit from our backyard: sweet mangoes, guavas, soft and delicious *nísperos*. We knew already that it was impossible to keep a true tally, because in a few minutes their number would increase from a handful circling over our heads to several dozens, coming and going, so that we were unable to tell which were the ones just leaving the nest. Counting them over and over again, we would finally give up and burst out laughing, at the bats, at ourselves, at our game, and at the delightful warmth of the night, fragrant with the aroma of jasmine and gardenias. My aunts and my mother would smile, and shake their heads: "There go those two, counting bats again . . ."

The quiet serenity of those evenings and the tender love my grandmother and I shared has nourished me often throughout my life. On the many occasions when I have later felt that I am once more trying to count bats, engaged in an impossible task, I have allowed myself to laugh, happy to remember that some of the best things in life are like counting bats: It was never the final count that mattered, but rather the joy of seeing them fly. ❧

CLAY

In the summer months, rain would often pour unannounced, pounding furiously on the treetops, the roof, and the soil. These summer rains provided wonderful fun for my mother and me. Together we would run outside in our bathing suits to play. It was wonderful to feel the strong drops on my bare back, to shake my head and feel my long hair wet and heavy with rainwater, to take off my rubber sandals and let the soft mud ooze between my bare toes.

But as much as I enjoyed the mud, I much preferred the clay, thick and red, which I gathered across the river to make toy dishes and cups. I would roll the clay into a ball and then press it between the palms of my hands until it became a round dish. To make a soup bowl, I would press hard in the center of a clay ball with both thumbs. I would make a cup by pressing a ball of softened clay against the palm of one hand to flatten the base. Then, with my index finger, I would slowly form a round cavity in the center. The handle was a long cylinder of clay, bent to create the right shape.

Usually I let my creations dry in the sun. But occasionally, the brick makers who worked on the other side of the river would let me put my own board, with my carefully made dishes, inside their oven. Sometimes the dishes would crack in the oven's strong heat, but some survived as the red clay turned black, strong, and durable.

Not just a plaything for a child, that same red clay was used for many useful products. Among the things that Camagüey is known for are *tinajones,* big-bellied clay pots. During colonial times, when there was no town water reservoir, every court-yard had one or more *tinajones.* In the rainy season, rainwater would stream down from the high tile roofs into the gutters, to be collected in the *tinajones* and preserved for the months in which there was no rain. Nowhere else in Cuba could such superb clay be found, nor potters able to create pots of that size. The potters had all disappeared by the time of my child-hood, but the clay, red and thick, was still abundant.

The few potters still willing to turn the wheel, with bare feet that wet the clay as it took form, made little *tinajones* to be sold as souvenirs to the few tourists who visited the town, but espe-cially to nostalgic former residents who had moved from Camagüey to Havana and wanted to decorate their new apart-ments and houses with memories of their old hometown.

The little *tinajones,* or *tinajoncitos,* were sold in different styles and sizes. Some were simply made of baked clay, others were glazed, and yet others were painted with small landscapes, perhaps of a solitary palm tree standing by a *bohío,* a thatched-roof cottage.

As children we took to school clay pots, round and heavy, with a small handle on top and a tiny hole to drink from. Although in Spain the same piece of pottery is called a *botijo,* we called them *porrón,* perhaps because it rhymes with *tinajón.* Time often brings changes quickly. The *porrón* was one of the things that I saw disappear during my own childhood. My sister Flor is only seven years younger than I, but she never carried a *porrón* to school. Instead, she drank out of a water fountain.

I have forgotten much of what I learned in school as a child. But how vividly I remember the lessons I learned from clay! Softening the clay was a tedious job. But only if it was soft enough could I mold it. Nothing could speed the process. Although water helped, one had to use just the right amount. Too much would make the clay slippery and impossible to shape. Working with clay taught me patience.

Since I could only use in the brick maker's oven occasionally, my little pots most often dried in the sun, which left them fragile but for that reason all the more precious. The things I shaped from clay taught me to treasure what I can create.

I have grown up to love pottery. Whenever I see a clay pot, I think of the women who throughout thousands of years have molded clay in their hands, to carry water, to store food, to cook and nourish their families. I like to imagine the first human being who discovered that clay could be shaped by human hands, and the many others who, in different parts of the world, arrived at the same discovery.

To me, life is a series of miracles, and the presence of this generous and elemental material around us—ready to be used for so many purposes, ready to be made into a thing of beauty—is one of those miracles.

How fresh and cool the water from the *porrón* tasted—pure water, with a slight flavor of clay! Water that had trickled through the stone filter in our kitchen as we slept. Water that my mother had lovingly poured for me that morning. A little bit of home for the long school hours. Friendly water, always waiting for us right next to our desks, during the heat of the day. ❦

EXPLORERS

Life at *La Quinta Simoni* provided constant invitations for adventure. One morning I met my cousins Jorge and Virginita by the fallen tree. It was a huge poplar, possibly uprooted by a hurricane. But the tree had refused to die and, although fallen, had sprouted new branches. These new branches, covered with heart-shaped leaves, projected upward like spears pointed at the sky. The tree was an excellent place for playing. Sometimes it became our pirate ship: On it, we crossed the Caribbean while the wind filled our green sails. At other times it was a castle, and from its turrets we defended our fortress from invading warriors. Or perhaps it was a covered wagon crossing the plains, or a sleigh racing across the Russian steppes pursued by a wolf pack. This day, the fallen tree was our camp, in the middle of the jungle, and from there we planned to go exploring.

Jorge instructed us on the importance of moving silently, crawling through the bushes, to evade the ferocious predators and fierce warriors who followed us. We were not to speak or ever to look behind us. If we dawdled or turned back, we might be eaten by wild beasts or captured by headhunters.

Virginita and I listened to him, fascinated. Not only was he two years older than his sister and four years older than I, he was the one who read the adventure stories that we all later reenacted. We trusted his words completely and followed him without hesitation.

We left behind the fallen tree and the chicken coop, where the hens were bathing themselves in the dust and eating the red berries from the *ateje* tree. We crept through the shadows of the flame trees, across the brilliant crimson carpet of their fallen petals, until we made it to the river.

We encountered no wild beasts or headhunters on our journey. On the contrary, our arrival merely prompted a few frogs and a turtle that had been sunning itself on a rock to jump into the water.

We crossed the river without any difficulty and sneaked around the brick maker's place. The old brick maker and his two sons, who had come from Spain after the Spanish Civil War, paid no attention to us. They were working barefooted. Their white trousers, which were made from flour sacks, were soiled with red clay. Their suntanned backs glistened with sweat. They were trying to loosen the iron wheel of the *pisa,* the round pit where the clay was broken and softened. The old skinny horse who made the wheel go around and around was

✦ MY MOTHER AND MY AUNT MIREYA ✦

IN THE GROUNDS OF THE OLD QUINTA SIMONI

waiting patiently, possibly thankful for having this brief rest under the sun.

Beyond the brick maker's place, the thorny bushes began. They say that the *marabú* plant was brought to Cuba by a countess who loved its flowers, which resemble pink powder puffs. But the bush did not want to remain locked up in a garden, so it slowly spread out across the fields.

Once *marabú* takes hold of a field, it is difficult to clear it. Its roots intertwine under the soil, forming a net that is almost impossible to pull out. One must plow the field to turn over the earth and then rake it, making sure that every last piece of root is removed. Otherwise, it will sprout again.

A *marabú* field is impenetrable unless a path is opened with a machete. The thorny branches form a barrier open only at ground level.

And it was at that level that we began to cross the *marabú* field. Jorge showed us how easy it could be if we simply crawled between and around the thin trunks. It was easy enough, indeed. But soon we had lost him. Because it was impossible to stand up or even to turn, we did not stop. Virginita and I continued, trying to follow the route plotted by our chief explorer, who was by now far ahead and out of sight.

Out in the countryside, people used the *marabú* to make charcoal. At that time in Cuba, very few people had electric or gas stoves. Poor people cooked with wood. Those who could afford it used charcoal. And the *marabú* charcoal was the best. *Marabú* is a very hard wood, so its coals last a long time before they are totally consumed.

To make *marabú* charcoal, the coal makers cut the trunks or the thickest branches and stripped them of leaves and thorns. Then they stood the wood on end, forming a shape much like a tepee. This structure was then covered with earth, with only a small opening left at the top. A fire was lit through an opening in the bottom. The *marabú* would then burn slowly, without flames, until it turned into charcoal. The oven had to burn for several days, and the coal makers would guard it day and night to be sure that it did not burn too fast.

Sometimes, if the oven was burning too fast, they had to open it and throw inside green wood or more dirt. It was not uncommon for the coal makers to carry terrible scars, evidence of how dangerous their job was.

As we moved farther into the *marabú* field, the trees seemed to grow closer and closer together, the branches more intertwined. The thorns caught on our dresses, tore at our hair. But there was nothing we could do. With Jorge's order never to turn back still fresh in our minds, and with a desperate desire to escape the *marabú* jungle, we struggled on, hoping to find our leader at some turn of the maze.

The coal makers sold their charcoal on the streets. Those who were more fortunate had a *plancha,* a primitive open wagon with four big wheels and no sides, on which they would place their charcoal sacks. The poorer ones would walk through the street with a half-full sack of charcoal slung over their shoulders, selling a handful of coal for the day's cooking to those who could not afford to buy a whole sack. They wore one of the coarse burlap sacks over their heads to protect their backs from the heavy burden.

For hours, Virginita and I crawled through the *marabú,*

avoiding when we could the dead thorny branches that had fallen on the ground, leaving behind pieces of our dresses and strands of our hair.

Meanwhile, at home, everyone was alarmed. The girls were lost! Jorge, who had returned a long time ago, had moved on to other pastimes. Nobody knew where to find us.

My parents went to the river. They talked to the brick makers. But not for a minute did they imagine we would have entered the *marabú* field. Jorge, to avoid a scolding, said only that he had left us playing at the other side of the river.

Late in the afternoon, with our clothes in tatters and our faces covered with muddy tears, we finally emerged at the other end of the *marabú* field. We were immediately surrounded by a group of children, half naked and as dirty as we were by then, who invited us to play hide-and-seek. Of course we were much too exhausted to accept.

Hearing us crying, the parents of the children appeared at the doors of their huts.

"Poor little ones," one of the women said kindly. "They are lost." She took me in her arms and asked Virginita to follow her.

With water from an old tin basin, she washed our faces and arms, all covered with scratches. Then she opened an old lard can, which she used as her cupboard, and took out two crackers—thick, large sailors' crackers. She sprinkled them with coarse brown sugar—poor people's way of fooling their bodies into believing they had eaten when there was no more substantial food to be had. Then she gave one to each of us.

"Eat, little ones, eat," she said, coaxing us. "Don't worry. We'll take you home."

✦ WITH UNCLE MARIO, AUNT LOLITA AND A COUSIN ✦
IN THE GROUNDS OF LA QUINTA SIMONI

And from the doorway, the children looked at us with big, open eyes, trying to imagine what we possibly could have done to merit such a generous and unexpected treat. ❦

BROKEN WINGS

My mother had three sisters but only one brother, Medardo. All four sisters were so outgoing, athletic, and daring, at a time when most women were not expected to be, that perhaps Medardo felt the need to live up to their example. Or maybe it was simply because he had been born with a surprisingly tall and strong body that Medardo grew up to excel in sports and succeed in all physical challenges. At a time when movies and comic books extolled such heroes, my uncle Medardo seemed to all of us to be a mixture of Tarzan and Superman.

Several times, he had braved the currents of the flooded Río Tínima to save someone from its muddy waters. He was the delight of the neighborhood boys because he would give them rides on his large nickel-chromed bicycle—six or seven of them at a time: one on the handlebars, one or two on the bar in front of him, two or three on the grill behind his seat, and, most dar-

✦ MY MOTHER AND HER THREE SISTERS ✦
AUNT VIRGINIA, AUNT MIREYA,
ALMA (MY MOTHER), AND AUNT LOLITA

ing of all, one perched on his shoulders. He would ride at full speed, as if he did not have to balance this human tower, and the boys would scream with delight and beg for yet another ride.

At other times, people riding the bus as it crossed the bridge over the Tínima would gasp with surprise and fear when they saw him on the high bridge, walking precariously on the railing like a circus acrobat.

Medardo loved adventures and wanted to explore any new frontier. Yet there was so little excitement in Camagüey! When he was twenty-four years old, he decided to learn to fly an airplane. He convinced a friend to join him, and each of them bought his own "flying machine," a primitive two-person plane, with a single motor and a precarious frame of light wood and canvas.

Medardo was by then married to his young bride, Geraldina, a beautiful brunette whom everyone said resembled Deanna Durbin, a Hollywood star at that time. They lived, as we did, in the big old *Quinta Simoni*. Their only child, my cousin Nancy, had just recently been born.

Neither his wife, nor my mother, nor my younger aunt Lolita, wanted Medardo to fly. My father tried to point out to him the risks involved and made every effort to divert him when Medardo came home from his work at a downtown office. But nothing could deter my uncle from the excitement that he felt while soaring, first behind the instructor, and then very soon afterward all by himself, rising above the red tile roofs, the winding streets that had so restricted his world, gliding like the mighty *auras*, the Cuban buzzards, over the plains where the royal palms stood majestically.

By the time Medardo got off from work on weekdays, it was usually too late to go flying. But on weekends, he never missed a single opportunity.

So, while he lived for the weekends, the rest of the family dreaded those Saturdays and Sundays. Secretly, without daring to admit it, I longed for the weekends, too. To me, what my uncle was doing was exciting. I felt both pride and joy that he would dare to defy all, including the force of gravity that keeps us all tied to the earth.

I had never yet been on an airplane, and it would be many years before I would fly. The closest I had come to flying was when my father pushed me hard on a swing he had tied to the high branch of a tree in the backyard. Or when, on clear nights, my father would place a blanket on the flat rooftop, and we would quietly gaze at the stars until it seemed that we were also floating in the galaxy. Oh, but to *really* fly! I could easily understand why Medardo would not give it up.

Torn between her fear and her own pride, my mother had agreed to embroider his jumpsuit with a pair of wings and his monograph, MLS, for Medardo Lafuente Salvador. The day had been dark and cloudy, as if a storm were approaching, and my mother and aunts had sighed with relief, thinking that at least that day he would not go flying.

But in the afternoon the sky cleared, and Medardo was determined to take wing.

My mother, busy at the sewing machine, kept arguing with him. He must wait patiently, she said, for her to finish the complicated embroidery on the back of the jumpsuit. But even I could see through her subtle ploy to keep him home. Medardo finally prevailed and forced her to give him the jumpsuit with only half of the embroidery done. "What I want is to fly." He tried to reassure her with a kiss. "You can finish the embroidery during the week."

A moment later, he jumped on a bus for the long trip to the airport at the other end of town. I played for a while, until my mother reminded me to take the shower that was part of my afternoon ritual. Then I could go out and sit on the porch, or collect flowers to make garlands, or wait for the neighborhood children who came to our porch to play.

But this afternoon there would be no games. I had only been in the bath for a few minutes, my body all covered with soap, my hair held high atop my head in a white cloud of shampoo, when I heard a noise like nothing I had ever heard. It was a thunder of human voices and running feet.

I climbed on the toilet seat to look out the bathroom window. There were hundreds of people running along the road in front of our house, heading toward the river. Everyone was shouting at once, so I could not understand what they were saying. But I did not wait. Without rinsing or drying myself, I put on the same dress I had just taken off and ran out barefoot.

Instead of going out into the street—the number of people there was frightening—I ran in the same direction, but behind the house, through the courtyard, down the lane lined with flame trees, and through the garden my great-grandmother loved so much.

By then I had figured out where everyone was heading and why. We were running in the same direction as an approaching plane, a plane that each moment grew larger as it loomed closer and closer to the ground, with a loud noise that was not the usual steady purr of a functioning motor, but the coughing and spitting of a motor incapable of holding the plane in the air.

As the plane passed above my head, I could see the big numbers and letters painted on the wings. It was NOT my uncle's plane! And yet, I kept running with the same energy, trampling the rosebushes that my great-uncle Manuel had cultivated to sell on the city streets, tearing my dress on the thorns.

And I was the first to reach the plane after the deafening impact. I was followed closely by my father, who quickly took me in his arms and pulled me away, but not before my eyes had filled with the terrible image I still remember today.

My father knew immediately there was nothing that could be done for my uncle, whose face had crashed forward against the control panel. His instinct was to protect me, to protect my mother, who was there now, wailing—how can someone cry with so much pain and anguish and horror!—my younger aunt, Lolita, who was holding her pregnant belly as if about to faint.

There were many hands to help lift the lifeless body from the plane. My aunt Geraldine, until that afternoon my uncle's wife and now his widow, was ushered into a car to hold on her lap the beloved head now unrecognizable.

How long and dark was that unbearable afternoon! The house was swarming with people. Some we knew, many were well-wishers, wanting to bring some comfort, but most were just curious onlookers.

✦ MY UNCLE MEDARDO ✦

MEDARDO LAFUENTE SALVADOR

To many in town we had always been an odd family. Living in a house reputedly haunted, all of us were looked on as eccentric. My grandfather Medardo was loved by his students and well-respected in intellectual circles. But to the ordinary people he was an odd gentleman who spoke as if reciting poetry and always walked with a book in his hand. They told funny anecdotes of having seen him so engrossed in his book as he walked that, upon bumping into a lamppost, he raised his hat, said "Excuse me," and continued walking.

An odd family, indeed. My grandmother Lola had been the first woman in town to cut her hair in a short page-boy fashion. That was unheard of in a grown woman with children, and a school principal at that. And my mother and my aunts had not only cut their hair too, they had also shortened their skirts and exposed their bare legs without stockings. They rode horses bareback, and drove cars and trucks.

Yes, indeed, we were odd. We were not even Catholic, in a town that was almost exclusively so. And it was not because we were Jewish or Protestant, either. My grandparents had simply chosen to believe in freedom of thought and spirit.

Now, to top it all off, my uncle had dared to fly one of those flying machines and . . . he had crashed!

No one held any grudges against us. We were known to be kind and generous. Even though any kindness was always shown quietly, people knew they could count on us.

But now, their curiosity had been stirred up. And there they were, the whole town, to see, to examine, to explore, to probe, to judge. . . . People whom we did not know felt they could enter the house. No space was sacred to them, no privacy was respected. This accident, and the grief that had torn the fabric of our own lives, became a spectacle like a circus.

My mother and my aunts cried loudly, wailing, letting their pain fill the house from which all joy had disappeared in an instant.

Five years earlier, my grandfather Medardo had died a painful but serenely accepted death, with his wife and children gathered around his bed. In his own room, he said good-bye as gently as he had always lived. He had simply asked for three teaspoons of water, saying, "For me, the time is here."

Two years later, my dear grandmother Lola had followed him, going forever peacefully in her sleep. In both instances, large crowds had come to the wake, waiting outside the house behind the black hearse pulled by black horses with tall black feather tufts, following it on foot all the way to the distant *camposanto,* the "holy field," or cemetery.

On both previous occasions, the crowds had been like the full and gentle swelling of the river after the summer rains. Now the mob was like the flood after a hurricane: uncontrollable, turbulent, sweeping away everything in its path.

My father and my uncle Manolo, my aunt Lolita's husband, were both stunned, having just lost their best friend. They were beset by the guilt of not having known how to prevent this disaster that all had feared. All their attention was now on their wives. My father, looking after my baby sister, Flor, who was still nursing, worried that my mother's milk would dry up. At a time when baby formula was not common, this was considered disastrous. My uncle Manolo worried about his pregnant wife, Lolita. And both were bewildered

✦ UNCLE MEDARDO AND AUNT GERALDINA ✦

about what to do with Geraldina, the young widow, who alternated between expressions of utmost grief and a pale and stiff rigidity in which she herself looked like death.

All over the house, people were trying to explain the accident in the most bizarre ways. The truth, which I learned later, was that because my uncle Medardo was delayed so long on the bus, his friend had decided to go ahead and fly by himself. But once aboard his own plane, he had trouble starting it. Thinking that Medardo was not going to show up at all, he went ahead and borrowed my uncle's plane. When Medardo got to the airfield, he found his plane gone. Believing it to be a prank, he took his friend's plane instead. This time the plane started fine, only to malfunction in mid-air.

Why did he choose the rose field next to our house for his crash-landing? Some people believed that he was showing off, that he had wanted to impress his wife. Most likely, he wanted to spare the town. He knew this field well. And yes, in moments of great despair, maybe one does try to get close to home.

For me, the speculation was useless and hurtful. What did it really matter? The unthinkable had happened. And my grief was heightened by my own unbearable secret. I could still hear my mother and my aunts repeating, over and over, between their bursts of sobbing and wailing, "We never wanted him to go," "We did all we could to dissuade him," "We tried to make him stop flying."

But only I knew that *I* had not wanted him to stop. Just that afternoon I had secretly rejoiced in seeing him so determined, overruling everyone in order to go out to his plane.

There was no possible consolation. I felt guilty, as if I had been the one to send him to his death. Of course, I had never believed that flying was as dangerous as everyone else seemed to think. But why had I not seen it? How could I have wanted him to fly when it was going to cause such pain?

What I did then is something I have kept secret for many years. I am telling it now because sharing one's hidden sorrows, those thoughts that we sometimes believe to be shameful, is a way to begin to heal our wounds. I am sharing this because as we hear each other's stories, we often begin to understand ourselves better and to feel less alone.

Riddled by my feelings of guilt, I rushed into my room, a room now invaded by strangers, and grabbed Heidi, my precious doll.

This doll was my truest friend. Heidi slept with me, kept me company, listened to all my thoughts and dreams. I carried her with me always, sharing every moment with her as two best friends would.

Now I ran with her in my arms to the back of the house. I knew my father's carpenter's bench well, and finding a hammer was not difficult. In the large courtyard, squatting behind the large masonry turret which led to the *aljibe,* the water cellar where rainwater was collected in colonial times, I placed Heidi on the tiled floor and smashed her head with the hammer, breaking that sweet little round forehead kissed so many times before, just as the plane's control panel had shattered my uncle's skull.

I hid the broken doll among the bushes, covering its small body with my tears and flower petals. Then I sat down next to one of the columns in the courtyard and silently cried myself to sleep.

I don't know who found me that night, or when or how I was taken to town. The next day, I found myself at my grandfather Modesto's house, walking aimlessly in the backyard.

I had forgotten all that had happened the day before, yet I felt the most powerful urge to go back to my own house. My uncle Mario, who had been left in charge of me, was not hard to persuade.

But getting home was a nightmare. All of the buses were packed with people heading in only one direction. Our sleepy town, where nothing ever happened, had been shaken by what was probably the most unexpected event since the War of Independence. When we finally arrived, the house was so full of people that only by crawling between their legs could I enter. Every horror of the previous day was now magnified in front of me.

I stopped at the door of the room where my uncle's body lay. There were my two older cousins, Jorge and Virginita. They had just arrived from Havana with their mother, Virginia, my oldest aunt. My aunt Virginia had joined her sisters at their brother's side, while my two cousins, like me, had not been able to enter the room where our mothers cried incessantly.

I held fast to each of them with both hands. I was shaking from fear and pain, and sweating from the efforts of pushing past so many people to get into my own house. I led in silence, and they followed me outside with the solidarity of our love and our mutual pain. Once outdoors, I pulled out my beloved

✦ THE HEARSE, READY TO TAKE MEDARDO TO THE CEMETARY ✦

doll from beneath the few leaves and petals I had used to cover her the night before. As I sat on the grass, rocking the broken doll one last time, my cousin Virginita put her arm around my shoulder while Jorge, having taken a shovel from the garden toolshed, dug the small grave. They accepted the broken doll just as they had accepted my uncle's death, without a question.

We shrouded the little body in a pillowcase. Virginita covered the bottom of the grave with flowers and Jorge placed the doll inside. Virginita and I brought some jasmine, carnations, and a few roses from the courtyard flower beds. Jorge continued to fill the grave with dirt until there was no more sign of Heidi, now forever lost to me in body, reduced to memory, just like our uncle.

Her softness and his strength, her smallness and his height, her silent acceptance of my kisses and his boisterous laughter while he lifted me up in the air, her quiet company and his exhilarating playfulness, all were now gone. Never again would I hold Heidi on my lap as I read a book beneath the flame trees, nor would I ride on my uncle's shoulders so high that I could pick the blossoms from those tall branches. And yet today, how alive in my memory are both my sweet gentle doll sacrificed by a hurting child, and my brave uncle, inviting me, every morning, to the untold adventure of a brand-new day. ❦

◆ ALMA FLOR ADA ◆

10 YEARS OLD

CHRISTMAS
FOR ALL

Until I was eight years old, my mother worked as an accountant for several small businesses. She would visit each store, collect the large ledgers and the voluminous envelopes filled with receipts, and bring them home. There she would spend many hours a day copying figures into the ledgers with her meticulous handwriting and adding the long columns of numbers. Then shc would return the thick ledgers and envelopes and collect new ones from her next client.

My mother was very proud of her profession. She had completed her education going to school at night after I was born, and was very proud of being one of the first women who was certified as a public accountant in Cuba.

After my sister Flor was born, my mother decided that she was ready to have her own business. She rented a garage from a typewriter repair shop in Calle Avellaneda and opened a small store where she sold buttons and lace, scissors and thread, needles and yarn, as well as paper, pencils, pens, and erasers. The customers tended to come in to the store at certain hours. Women came in the morning, on their way home from the market. Students came in the afternoon, right after being let out from school. Young women came in the evening, on their way to night classes. No matter who they were, my mother always had a word of wisdom or encouragement for them, or a joke to make them laugh. Sometimes I suspect the customers came into the little store more for my mother's words than for the little trinkets they bought—especially the young women who came for a pad of paper or a pencil, but also asked my mother to go over their homework or explain a difficult math problem.

In the quiet hours of midday, my mother kept doing her accounting work, leaning on the countertop while she waited for a customer—a lady to browse among the lace, or a harried maid to select a zipper, or a young boy to buy a jar of glue to make a kite.

My baby sister, Flor, was kept in a large cardboard box which served as a makeshift playpen, and I did my homework sitting on the tile floor, grateful for its coolness in the hot afternoon.

One day my mother surprised everyone at home: my father, her younger sister Lolita, and Lolita's husband, Manolo, whom I called Tío Tony to distinguish him from my father's brother who was also named Manolo.

There had been a lot of talk of late about of how difficult it was for the two young couples remaining to keep up the big

Quinta Simoni. In a few years both my grandparents and my uncle Medardo had died. My two other aunts, Virginia and Mireya, had gone to work and live in Havana. And the big old house was expensive to run.

But my mother had an idea that was quite a surprise. She suggested they could all together purchase an old jewelry store that was for sale in the center of town.

It did not take long to convince the others. Here was an opportunity to have a business and to live on the premises. That would ease the economic situation. Also, I suspect that the large, rambling *Quinta Simoni* reminded them of how much they missed those who were no longer living with us.

So shortly afterward we moved to Calle República, to the house behind the Joyería El Sol, a few blocks away from the little store that had been my mother's first business venture.

For me, it was a most difficult time. I loved the old *Quinta Simoni*, where I had been born. I loved its large rooms with high ceilings, the flat roof, where my father and I would lie gazing at the night sky while he told me stories about the constellations. I loved the pigeons and guinea pigs my aunt Lolita raised, and above all, my friends the flame trees, with their gnarled roots where I sat as if in the lap of my grandfather.

I realize that perhaps the house made the adults sad, after the deaths of my grandfather Medardo, my grandmother Lola, and my young uncle Medardo. But for me, they were still alive. I felt their presence in the hallways, on the porch and in the courtyard. All during the four years in which we lived in the city, I longed to return to live among the trees.

The only good times in the city, for me at least, were the

feast of San Juan in June, which was celebrated almost like a Mardi Gras, and of course Las Navidades, or Christmastime.

As soon as they bought the Joyería El Sol, my family began to make improvements to the old jewelry store. My father, always ready to learn new things, learned how to fix watches. My mother, lover of innovations, had the storefront redone with large display cases. She also began to display a wider variety of merchandise.

The old jewelry and stopwatches were relegated to a few special counters. The other displays were filled with porcelain and crystal. During the first Christmas season, my mother brought in toys and the traditional figurines used to create Nativity scenes.

It was a Cuban tradition, common also in Spain and other Latin American countries, to set up a Nativity scene in the house during the month of December. It was a tradition shared by rich and poor alike, although the elaborateness of the scene varied greatly from home to home. More than a family's economic status, it was their willingness to make an effort, to set aside space, and to be creative that determined the size and originality of the scene.

The mountainous backdrop for the scene could be constructed with cardboard boxes covered with paper grocery sacks. The sand for the desert was brought in from a trip to the beach. The fields could be created by sprouting wheat in small cans or jars; a piece of broken mirror provided the surface for a lake. The figurines, though—the shepherds and their lambs, the three Wise Men, Mary, Joseph, and Jesus, the donkey and the cow—were usually store-bought.

✦ MY FATHER ✦

MODESTO ARTURO ADA REY

My mother imported some figurines from Spain. They were made of clay and set in elaborately detailed and realistic settings carved out of cork. We cherished unpacking them, carefully lifting them from layers and layers of straw to discover the minute details of a kitchen with an old woman by the fire, a mother breast-feeding her baby, a young girl spinning wool. Each one was a unique, handmade piece. But these figurines were very expensive, and very few people could afford them.

My mother then set out to find another source. In Havana she discovered an Italian artist who produced beautiful ceramic figurines. I still remember his name, Quirico Benigni, because he was the first Italian I had ever met. His figurines were carefully crafted, but they were made in series, not individually, so they were somewhat less expensive.

Even so, many people came into the store and handled the figurines, observed their beauty with a smile, but returned them to the shelves after seeing the price. And there were those who would not even enter the store, but simply looked longingly through the windows.

Then my father sprang into action. Though we were not Catholic, he understood the joy people found in re-creating the Nativity scenes. He considered it a creative project, in which every member of a family, young or old, could participate. And he decided we, too, would also have a family project, one that would make Nativity figurines accessible to all.

First he enlisted my aunt Lolita's artistic talent and had her model in clay each of the major figures of the Nativity scene: Mary, Joseph, the Baby, the three Wise Men, the donkey, and the cow. Then he constructed a series of hinged wooden boxes, each a little bigger than the figurines. He filled one side of each box with plaster of paris. Before the plaster hardened, he took one of the clay figurines, covered it with grease, and submerged one whole side of it into the plaster.

Once the plaster hardened, he removed the clay model, which had left an imprint in the plaster. He then repeated the same procedure with the other side of the box, and the other side of the model.

Through this simple process, he created a series of molds. Now we could grease the inside of each mold, close and lock the hinges, and pour in soft plaster of paris through a hole in the bottom of each box.

My father made several attempts until he determined how much time the plaster needed to harden in the molds. Then he was ready to operate. Several times a day, he would open his molds and take out the white figurines, which he set out to finish drying on the patio wall.

Every evening, after the little ones, my sister and cousin, had gone to sleep, the whole family would gather together to work on the figurines.

It was my duty to clean with a knife the excess plaster that collected along the figurines' sides, where the two halves of the mold met. My mother then gave them a first coat of paint that colored Mary's mantle blue, the robes of the Wise Men red or green, the shepherd's cassocks brown.

Lastly, my aunt Lolita carefully painted their features with small brushes until the white plaster was all covered and the figurines became recognizable characters.

My uncle Manolo, Tío Tony, would prepare the plaster, clean the molds, and more than anything else, entertain us all with his unending stories.

The next day, some humble hands would happily exchange a few pennies for one of the figurines, which we had placed on a table by the door of the store, and take it home to add to their Nativity scene.

The pennies barely covered the cost of the materials, let alone the time spent by my parents or my aunt. In fact, the figurines were not very artistic, nor terribly graceful, I must confess. But we saw them go with the hope that they would bring others the same joy we had shared as we labored into the night together, believing that this was the essence of Christmas: a celebration in which all can take part, and find a way to express their love for one another. ❈

GILDA

School became enjoyable for me for the first time at the beginning of fourth grade, thanks to my teacher, Gladys Carnero.
Gentle, loving, and interesting, her enthusiasm for teaching
made us all want to learn.

When midway through the school year she moved to
Havana, I felt lost. Then I became sick. First I caught one cold
after another, then the measles, and finally the mumps. My
wonderful parents realized that something lay beneath this.
The *Colegio Episcopal* which I had been attending was unbearable to me if Gladys Carnero was no longer there. So, my parents transferred me to a new school.

Although it might have been a relief at the beginning of the
school year, this transfer became another kind of nightmare. I
arrived as the new child in the middle of the year—to a class
where all of the other children had known each other since

✦ WITH MY VIOLIN ✦

9 YEARS OLD

first grade. To make it worse, at the new school, *Colegio El Porvenir,* the students were seated according to their academic performance. Those with the best grades sat in the front; those with bad grades sat in back. Since I had no grades yet, they sat me at the very back.

In the last row, I was surrounded mostly by boys who were the tallest in the class. I, a year younger than my classmates, was the shortest. Furthermore, no one had discovered yet that I needed glasses. I could not see anything on the board.

And the final blow was that the two previous schools I had attended were American schools, where they taught mathematics, especially division, very differently from the Cuban schools. So although I knew how to find the right answer, I couldn't explain how I did it. Was I lost!

Those first few months at the *Colegio El Porvenir* were not easy. I couldn't find any reason to be there. The teacher would write a sentence on the board, and we were supposed to analyze it, identifying the subject and the predicate, the direct object and the indirect object. We had to identify the verb tense: present perfect, past perfect, pluperfect. I would say to myself, "What is this for? How is it possible that everyone else understands it and I don't?"

I tried to hide behind one of the students who sat in front of me, but it seemed that my strategy only brought me harder questions from the teacher. "Indicative," "subjunctive," and "imperative," sounded equally horrible to me. I loved words like "zephyr" and "zenith," "nectar" and "ambrosia," "friendship" and "loyalty." But the words "preposition," "conjunction," and "subordinate" sounded almost as ugly as "sulfur" and "hate" to me.

Because my parents had been so understanding, I felt I could not tell them how unhappy I was. There was only one thing that allowed me to survive that horrible school with its treeless cement yard—a school without songs, without drawing, without stories, without friends.

On my way to school one day, a couple of blocks down a side street that I had followed just to delay my arrival, an unexpected wisp of music greeted me, merrily escaping from a tall window behind a carved wooden railing.

On tiptoes, grasping the wooden railing, I peered inside the old colonial house from which the waltz spilled onto the street.

Inside, an enormous mirror reflected a dozen young girls, in pink leotards and black slippers, practicing at the barre. At the piano an older woman played the unending waltz. In front of the class, holding a tall staff, stood a young blond woman, so pale she was almost translucent. She had incredible eyes— eyes that took in everything: the girls, the piano player, and indeed the whole room, including the far corner where a group of elegant ladies sat in mahogany rocking chairs, sleepily cooling themselves with silk fans.

As the days went by, school became bearable only because as soon as the long-awaited bell rang, I would run and cling to the window of the ballet school, imagining myself in soft slippers, changing positions, second, third, fourth, performing a *jeté* or a *plié*.

One afternoon, the pale teacher disappeared from view, and before I realized what was happening, she was standing on the sidewalk by my side. "Do you want to study ballet? What is your name?"

Her voice was as soft as her gaze. "Come in," she said. "Come in."

Once she knew who I was, she called my mother and offered to accept me in her class. My life was changed, not only after school, but in school, too!

I was never again bothered by prepositions and conjunctions, nor by my inability to remember how much is seven times eight. Nor did I mind anymore sitting in the back of the class, although slowly, without really noticing how, I managed to move to the middle rows and even to the front.

I lived only for the moment when the bell rang and I could run to the ballet school. And it wasn't that I did very well there. I did not. I was placed at the end of the line, and there I stayed for as long as my classes continued. In spite of my love for music and for the beauty of the movements, it was as if I had three feet, or as though my left and right sides had traded places. But in spite of my clumsy attempts, so devoid of grace, how wonderful it was to be there!

No matter what mistake I made, I was never criticized nor ridiculed by Gilda, the teacher. Although I saw her become impatient once in a while, it was only when someone who could naturally do better was not paying attention. To me she offered the same gentleness she showed the youngest of the girls, looking at me with a sweet look of complicity, as if to say, "You know that I know you cannot dance, but that you long to be here, and I welcome you."

I was very surprised when one day my teacher invited me to stay after class. That was the beginning of a beautiful friendship that was cherished equally by both of us.

From that day on, at the end of class, we would go to the *saleta*, the informal sitting room and the coolest room in the house. The *saleta* opened to the courtyard, where the *tinajones,* huge clay jars, overflowed with fresh water, and jasmine filled the air with its delicate fragrance. Gilda would show me her scrapbooks filled with photos, newspaper articles, and programs, in Russian, French, and Italian. She had studied in Russia and had danced in Vienna, Münich, Amsterdam, Paris, and Rome.

Those names evoked worlds that I could barely imagine, far from the insignificant city of Camagüey. But more than the stories of ballets and parties, of triumphs and travels, I was fascinated by Gilda, by the life energy concentrated in that body, so fragile and delicate. She was to me a goddess I had the privilege to know.

At the end of the school year we had a recital at the *Teatro Principal,* and Gilda invited me to go see the theater with her before the recital. She showed me backstage, all the while telling me stories of the many theaters she had known. What an intriguing world it was backstage!

To see her dancing on the stage was a revelation. After my ballet classmates and I concluded our simple presentation, the master of ceremonies announced a number that was not on the printed program. Gilda would interpret Stravinsky's *Firebird.* For as long as I had known her, she had always been sweet and melancholic, filled with dreams, a romantic person. Now, as she became the music on the stage, the Gilda I knew disappeared, reincarnated as passionate strength, as vibrant determination. But the beautiful dance was not to be, as she fainted on the stage, unable to finish the piece.

Someone called an ambulance, and I saw her for the last time—a wounded bird, the bright yellow *lamé* dress like a dying flame draped over the white gurney.

Then came the rumors. She had cancer, the horrible sickness no one wanted to mention. By now it was summer and I did not have to go to school, but I walked many times the well-known route, stopping in front of the old colonial house that was now always closed.

When I was not out walking, I lingered around the jewelry store my parents had bought when we moved to town. There I heard Gilda had gotten married. Yet every comment related to the wedding was filled with sarcasm. "To marry Mr. Charles, who is at least forty years her senior!" "What a shame!" "How absurd!" "How obscene!" And these verbal attacks were accompanied by looks and gestures of disgust.

In our town there was never much to talk about, so any news was discussed over and again. Whenever anyone made a comment about Gilda's wedding, I would leave and go to our house behind the store. I felt unable to reconcile her marriage to an old French professor, who had visited her occasionally and whom she treated like a father, with the romantic nostalgia she exuded as she told me of the ballets she had danced. But I was also unable to accept that anyone else had the right to criticize what they did not understand. And at a deeper level, I felt abandoned.

I longed to see Gilda, and yet I did not know how.

Soon, it became public knowledge that she was again very sick, that she was dying, that it only would take a few days. One morning I overheard my mother saying to a friend that she did not know how to tell me the bad news. That whole day I hid in the backyard, under the *guanábana* tree, so that no one would try to tell me what I already knew.

That afternoon, my parents went out. I threw myself on my bed, pretending to read a book, unable to cry for something that seemed remote and unreal, but also unable to feel, to think.

Coralia, the old woman who had been my mother's nanny, came to tell me that there was a gentleman looking for me. At ten years old, I was not used to having gentlemen callers. But on that strange day, anything was possible. Shy, uncertain of how to talk to me, Mr. Charles held his hat in his hands, his white head tipped down onto his chest.

"Are you Almita Flor? Do you know me? We have seen each other at her house, haven't we?"

Those words, "her house," so filled with love in his voice, so filled with tenderness in my memory, prevented me from uttering anything in return. Instead, I nodded.

"She asked me to bring you this," he said, as unable to use the beloved name Gilda as I was of speaking. And he took from behind his hat a photograph of Gilda, dressed as the Firebird.

"She did not want you to see her when she was so ill," he explained patiently. "She wanted you to remember her as you knew her . . ."

And then he bent over and hugging, we cried, the old man and the child, for the broken flight of that gentle bird we had both loved, each of us so differently and yet so truly. ❧

MADAME
MARIE

"It will help bring in customers," I heard my mother telling my father. "She won't take up too much space, but above all I would like to help her, after all she has been through!"

"By all means," my father answered, "invite her to exhibit whatever she has to sell. Poor woman!"

The following day, upon returning from school, I saw in the old jewelry store the French lady. It was difficult for me to imagine that the person my parents had been talking about with such pity could be this tall woman with such a beautiful face and flaming red hair. She moved with grace and elegance behind a counter filled with embroidered tablecloths.

Shortly thereafter her two sons began attending our school. We were used to having people from Camagüey move to Havana; the only people who moved to Camagüey from other places came from the countryside, from towns even smaller than ours. That Jacques, the son who became my classmate, came from France was certainly a novelty. All of the boys wanted to talk to him, to learn more about his homeland. But they were met with silence. Jacques was only interested in studying, in improving his Spanish, and in turning in long, clean, meticulously finished homework assignments.

Soon the boys' interest turned into antagonism. And Jacques became the target of teasing and of practical jokes. We looked on from the side, some of us girls feeling ashamed, others laughing at the jokes to win a smile or an approving look from a boy.

Little by little, I heard the story at home, piecing it together like a puzzle from a phrase heard here and a comment there.

Madame Marie, as everyone called her, was a French woman. Just before the beginning of World War II she had met Felipe, a young man from Camagüey who had gone to study engineering in Paris. They had married soon afterward. Two boys were born to the couple, and they had decided to stay in France. They moved to the town where Marie's relatives lived. There they rented a large farmhouse from one of Marie's uncles. The house was surrounded by orchards, and Marie planted a vegetable garden and colorful flowers.

Being in the countryside, they were not overly concerned when the war began; but once France was occupied by the Nazis, they became terrified. Beautiful Marie, with her green eyes and flaming hair, was Jewish. Her father had been Catholic, but her mother, Judith, was born Jewish, and therefore Marie was considered Jewish also. Meanwhile, the Nazis were hunting down all Jewish people and sending them to concentration camps.

Felipe conceived a plan. He told all of his neighbors and relatives that he was sending his wife and children to Cuba until the war ended. They loaded the car with suitcases and, after saying good-bye to everyone, left in broad daylight for the next city. But in truth, Marie and the children spent the day hiding in the woods. That night, under the cover of darkness, they returned home through the fields.

Felipe hid them in a closet and covered the door with a heavy armoire. They would hide there all day long, in case the Nazis came to search the farm. In the evening, Felipe would move the armoire so they could walk through the dark house.

But after some time, Marie's uncle, the owner of the farm, demanded that Felipe put up another family in the house. Although he was the brother of Marie's father, he had never liked Judith, nor had he ever accepted that his nephew had married a Jewish woman.

Now, the uncle was convinced that the French people should collaborate with the Nazis, in order to prevent retaliation against France. Felipe knew he could not trust him with his secret nor the people he had brought to the farm.

Then the situation grew worse. Once the new family had moved into the house, Felipe could no longer open the closet at all. Fortunately, he had managed to keep as his bedroom the room with the closet, but he could not move the heavy armoire without making noise. So he only dared to move it when everyone was out, and even then not for very long.

Often Marie and the two boys were locked in for days or even for weeks on end, daring only to open the little window

Felipe had cut at the back of the armoire to pass them food and to take out the waste.

During all that time, Marie taught her children their lessons. She told them all she knew about the countryside, everything about planting and gathering that she had learned as a child. She told them about the history of France, and the history of the Jewish people. Very softly she would sing lullabies to them, nursery rhymes, the love songs she had heard on the radio, the music she had danced to with Felipe. And when she had sung those songs over and over, she created her own songs, about a world at peace, a land with no violence, where children were free and happy, where people united in solidarity and love for one another.

Whenever I came back from school, Madame Marie would rub little drops of perfume behind my ears and gently squeeze my shoulder, encouraging me to go practice on the violin. "*Mon petite, mon petite,* music is a great friend," she would say to me in her caressing voice. I do not know if she ever noticed my adoring gaze as she, with a smile softly curving her closed lips, organized over and over her small display of embroidered table clothes, napkins, and handkerchiefs in a corner of my mother's store. ❦

UNCLE
MANOLO'S
MYSTERY

My father's older brother, my uncle Manolo Ada Rey, was a shadowy figure during the early years of my childhood. He lived in Havana, where he had gone to study medicine. There he had married and begun his practice. Although we went to Havana twice a year, we always stayed with my mother's sister, my aunt Lolita, and only saw my uncle Manolo for what always felt like a very formal visit. Often, when people spoke about my uncle, the conversation seemed to be filled with long, strained silences.

In contrast to the homes of everyone else in the family, my uncle's house seemed gloomy to me. It was in the old part of town, commonly known as *La Habana Vieja* or Old Havana. The door and windows were kept shut to keep out the street noise and pollution. Since Manolo and his wife had no children, no pets, and no plants, and the house itself was old and musty, it was hard to look forward to going there, except for the great kindness that I perceived in my uncle's bespectacled eyes, and the unquestionable pleasure my father derived from seeing him.

I don't remember ever having a conversation with my uncle during all those years. As soon as we arrived for our afternoon visit, my sister and I would be entrusted to my uncle's wife and her mother. My aunt Isabel was a nurse, a very thin and nervous woman, who would exclaim as we arrived, *"¡Pobrecito!" "¡Pobrecita!,"* "Poor dear ones!"—implying that we must have had a long and tiring journey. Then she would pat my little sister gently on the head, exclaiming, *"¡Qué bonita, pobrecita!"* as though being pretty was something to be sad about.

Her mother was a country woman from northern Spain. She was a large, kind woman with a sad smile and teary eyes, who would bring us milk and cookies, and more cookies, and more milk, as if feeding us was her only way of telling us she cared.

I was a little intimidated by both of them, and wished that they would ask me questions the way other adults did, instead of pressing more milk and cookies on me.

Meanwhile, my mother and father carried on what I imagined to be a fascinating conversation with my uncle. The topic always seemed to be politics, and I tried to listen, although I could hardly make out the words over the sighs of my aunt and her mother, exclaiming for the hundredth time that my braids were so much longer than the previous year.

I don't know why I felt that the conversations with my uncle were so important. They certainly seemed to be so for

✦ UNCLE MANOLO ✦

MY FATHER'S OLDER BROTHER

my father, who looked invigorated by them. And I always wondered why we spent so much time with my mother's family and so little time with my father's.

More surprising to me still was that among my mother and her sisters, my uncle Manolo—so serious, so dignified behind his round tortoiseshell glasses—was spoken of in the same tone that my aunt Isabelita used when she called my sister and me *"¡Pobrecitas!"*

"They never travel," my aunts would comment, with the self-assurance of having visited Florida and New York themselves.

"They never go anywhere," they would add, "all they do is work and stay in that horrible house."

And then someone would make the comment that silenced everyone, as though there was nothing more that could be said: "And to have chosen not to have children!"

At this point, someone would usually glance in my direction. As the oldest child present, I might be starting to catch on to things. The speaker would be hushed with a vague comment, "Well, considering . . ."

A shadow of mystery hung over it all. A shadow easily forgotten on the many exciting days during those trips to Havana: a visit to the newly constructed zoo, with the beautiful statue of a deer at the front gate; evening strolls along the *Malecón*, the boardwalk by the ocean, watching huge waves crashing and turning into cascades of foam while we licked ice-cream cones in fabulous island flavors—coconut, mango, *guanábana, níspero*. There were wonderful days at the beach, at nearby Santa María del Mar, in Guanabo, or even farther away in Varadero, with its incomparable sand.

There were excursions by ferry to El Morro Castle, the old Spanish fortress on the other side of the bay. There we could see the impressive stone walls, thick and imposing, built to withstand the cannons of pirate ships and of the British navy. There were turrets to climb, and dungeons that made us gasp, and deep inside of us the proud secret that my own grandfather Medardo had been imprisoned here for having denounced the dictator Machado's tyranny in his newspaper. At that time, no one had told me yet that the terrible imprisonment had destroyed his health. Everyone wanted to forget and, even more so, to keep the children from knowing that he had suffered torture and hunger. So I simply gloried quietly in the secret of his heroism.

And then at last it was time for good-byes to aunts, uncles, and cousins, the long train or bus ride home through valleys studded with royal palms, proudly waving their *pencas*, their fronds, in the wind.

On one occasion my mother and my sister left earlier, driving home in my aunt Mireya's car. My father and I stayed behind to return home on the train. He had some business to finish in the old center of town. As usual, as we walked he urged me to look up and observe the elaborate facades of buildings decorated with fabulous statues, cornices, and cornucopias, now soiled by smog and dust and sometimes obscured by neon signs and political advertisements.

After my father finished his errands, he suggested that we visit his own aunt and uncle. Since I had never heard them mentioned before, this came as a surprise to me. I was excited because everything I did with my father–from trips to the countryside to stargazing–was always filled with revelations.

My father's aunt Isela and her husband lived out of town. As we waited on a busy corner, watching one overcrowded bus after another pass without stopping, my father began to tell me about his aunt Isela and her husband. In the process, he revealed the mystery of my uncle Manolo.

"My aunt and uncle never had any children of their own," my father began. "My aunt, my mother's younger sister, had lived with us when my brothers and I were little. She loved children and missed having a child around the house. So they decided to adopt a little girl from the *Casa de Beneficencia.*"

I knew this old orphanage, which stood on Calle Belascoaín, right across from my aunt Mireya's house. Since my aunt lived on the third floor, I had often watched from the balcony the children playing in the large courtyard of the old building.

My father continued, "All went well for a few years. They loved the little girl as their very own, and were very happy to have her. But when she became a teenager, something terrible happened."

His voice became very sad, and I waited expectantly. Just then a bus stopped, and a large group of people got off. We crowded our way in, my father protecting me with his outstretched arms. For quite a few blocks we rode standing up, squeezed in among so many bodies. But as the bus moved farther away from the city, my father was able to steer us to the rear, where we finally managed to sit down.

I could not wait to ask him, "What happened that was so terrible?"

"What happened," he answered me, "is that they discovered that the girl had a terrible, terrible illness.

"It is an old illness that humans have known for a very long time. It has always been thought to be incurable, and even worse, highly contagious. It is an illness called leprosy."

I was puzzled when I heard the word. I had heard it before, but I had always thought of it as happening in faraway places or at least in faraway times. I had read about Rodrigo Díaz de Vivar ("El Cid"), the brave Castilian knight who fought against the Moors for the independence of his homeland. Rodrigo, who was always so just that his own enemies had given him the name *Mio Cid,* "My Lord," had once taken off his gauntlet to shake the hand of a leper. Many considered this the bravest of his deeds. In my own hometown there was a legend about the old lepers' home, *Asilo de San Lázaro,* which was still standing. But now only elderly people who were homeless lived there, and I had thought that there was no leprosy left in Cuba.

"How horrible!" was all I could say.

"Yes," agreed my father, and continued. "They did not know what to do. The medical doctors told them not only that there was no hope for a cure, but that by law she needed to be hospitalized.

"It was very difficult for them to part with the girl they had loved so much. So they moved to where they now live. Their house is right across from the lepers' hospital.

"Visits to the hospital are rather restricted. But living across the road, my aunt could talk to her daughter through the fence, see her in the yard playing or talking with other girls.

✦ WITH AUNT MIREYA ✦

UNDER THE FLAME TREES, 1938

And she could bring her food from home, her favorite fruits, a special dessert.

"The director and the hospital staff were touched by such devotion. Many relatives of lepers push them out of their minds once they are institutionalized. The longer the lepers are in the hospital, the fewer visits they receive.

"The doctors were also very careful to warn my aunt of the probabilities of contracting the disease. My aunt simply reminded them they were taking even greater risks. Impressed by her courage and devotion, they opened their doors to her. She could come any day, at any time.

"And she did. She became the confidante of the girls. She listened to their sadness, their anger, their pain, and their dreams. She talked to the young men, to the older patients, and became their friend. She kept track of birthdays and brought homemade delicacies to be shared by all whose birthdays fell in the same month. She donated her own radio, since she was never home to listen to it anyway, and listening to the radio became one of the few pleasures they all could share. She collected old magazines and day-old newspapers for them, although the people who lived close to the hospital had themselves very little to spare.

"But it was probably her smiles, her words, and the fact that she saw them as the people they were, not as sick people, that made them love her so much.

"No matter how much the leprosy began to deform and destroy her daughter's body, she always talked about her beauty, because she could truly see past the sick body to the person she so dearly loved."

I was listening spellbound when the story took a surprising turn.

"My brother Manolo," my father added, "had always wanted to be a doctor. When our mother got sick and died, his decision was confirmed. As soon as he finished high school at the Instituto in Camagüey, he asked my father to let him apply to the University of Havana.

"He went to live in a boarding house in Vedado, near the university, and concentrated very hard on his studies. Feeling homesick for family, he searched out our aunt Isela. In the years since our mother's death, our aunt had always sent us letters at Christmas and on our birthdays. She always sent regards from her daughter and told us what a beautiful and sensitive person she was. I even suspect that on his first visit, my brother Manolo was not only hoping to see our aunt whom he had not seen in a long time, but also to meet this lovely cousin.

"At first he was appalled at discovering what my aunt had not been willing to reveal in her letters. He confessed to me that nothing in medical school had prepared him for the deformity and pain he saw on his first visit to the leper's hospital. But after that first visit, he could not stop thinking about it. "I know now," he told my aunt and her husband on his next visit, "why I truly wanted to become a doctor. And I know where I will practice."

"They listened with love and understanding, neither encouraging nor discouraging him. And he did not mention it again. But on the few occasions Manolo went out with a girl, he would let her know of his plans. Some tried to talk him out

✦ AUNT ISABEL ✦

WIFE OF UNCLE MANOLO

of it, others laughed nervously and refused to go out with him again.

"So he decided he would never get married. But a nurse in the Hospital Calixto García, where the medical students did their internships, had noticed the bright, quiet student. She was a little older than he but so slightly built that she looked younger than her years. When they met for an occasional cup of coffee, usually on the nights he was on duty and after she had finished her shift, she would ask him about his plans and listened as he talked about the lepers, their pain, their isolation, their abandonment.

"Finally she asked him once, 'When are you going there next?' And when he told her, she asked to go with him. So Manolo and Isabel's first date was a visit to the leper's hospital," my father said, almost as if explaining it to himself. "On the way home, he asked if she would marry him and she accepted. 'Provided that we agree not to have children. I could not bear the fear of passing this illness to a child. Let the patients be our children.'"

And so at last I learned the secret that made people hush every time they talked about my uncle Manolo and my aunt Isabel. My aunt and uncle were not lively and witty, funny and spirited like my mother's family, but their reserved exterior concealed an open and giving heart. ❦

THE LEGEND
OF THE WHITE
BUZZARD

The old house in which I was born, the *Quinta Simoni*, and the tiny house next to it where my great-grandmother lived were the last two houses on the *Calle General Gómez*, just before the road reached the river Tínima. On the banks of the river stood the radio station *Voz del Tínima*, owned by my grandfather Modesto, and a tall bridge spanned the gorge below.

One could spend hours looking down at the river from the bridge and I often did, watching the ducks dive for food, or glide swiftly and gracefully across the water. I observed the herds of goats, black on white, white on black, grazing along the riverbank. On the other side of the river was the smithy, where sweaty men wearing leather aprons shaped horseshoe after horseshoe, or held between their knees the folded leg of the horse they were shoeing.

Walking beyond the bridge one found a few scattered houses, a corner grocery store, the *Cuartel Agramonte,* the military barracks, and finally two institutions, an orphanage for boys and a home for elderly people, the *Asilo de San Lázaro.* Formerly, this had been a house for lepers, around which had grown a legend beautifully recorded by our own Tula.

Tula was Gertrudis Gómez de Avellaneda, an idol for some of us young girls in Camagüey. Born in Camagüey in 1814, she moved to Spain as a young woman when her widowed mother married a Spaniard. In Madrid she published poetry and plays, had an adventurous romance, and became one of the literary giants of the Romantic period. She never forgot Cuba, and her love for the island of proud royal palms appears over and over throughout her work. Later in life she returned to her homeland, if not to her hometown. It was very exciting to me to have been born in the same town as this great woman writer.

Her legend of the white buzzard, *el aura blanca,* fascinated me because I knew the places she was talking about, which truly had not changed very much in the past hundred years. Yes, now there were electricity, telephones, and cars, but essentially it was still a very quiet town, where most people knew each other, where stores closed at midday so that people could rest during *siesta* time, where the same festivities were held year after year, and where still some had plenty while others begged on the streets.

One thing that had changed is that there were no lepers living at the *Asilo de San Lázaro* any longer; now only old people lived there. Next to those who begged for pennies on the streets, they seemed well taken care of, despite their lonely look.

The *Asilo de San Lázaro* had originally been founded by a well-meaning priest, *Padre Valencia,* to make a home for the numerous lepers who roamed the outskirts of the city.

This generous man gave his life to the lepers, both ministering to them, and begging on their behalf. He was an eloquent speaker, and his heart was so touched by the pain of those he served that he managed to touch the hearts of others. Whenever he preached in town, he was able to collect the money that allowed him to build, slowly but steadily, his *Asilo.*

Padre Valencia spent nothing on himself. To strengthen his own spirit, he practiced the life of an ascetic, sleeping on two boards supported by a few bricks on the floor, with another brick as a pillow.

Daily he would walk through the town, knocking on doors, asking for charity for the lepers. And while he lived, the lepers lacked nothing. But even holy men die. After a long life of caring for others, Padre Valencia died.

Other priests took over his role, but they did not possess Padre Valencia's eloquence, nor his determination to walk the streets. And so the alms diminished and all but disappeared. Finally, convinced that it was impossible to keep the *Asilo* going, the priests departed as well. Only the lepers remained, the hungry, abandoned lepers.

And then one morning, as the unfortunate men and women gathered sadly in the courtyard to contemplate another day of misery, a surprising bird landed in their midst.

Cuba, rich in small wildlife, has an abundance of buzzards, known as *auras.* They can be seen on almost any day, soaring high, enormous wings spread wide, ebony black against the sky, searching for the dead animals on which they feed.

People know these birds are useful, since as scavengers they help keep the countryside clean. And while they are not exactly beautiful, up in the sky they are quite majestic.

The large bird that appeared among the lepers was indeed an *aura*. But two things were most surprising: It had descended there among them with no apparent fear, a very unusual behavior. And the second was that this *aura,* unlike the ones seen frequently in the sky, was completely white.

"A miracle! A miracle!" the lepers cried. "Just as I was thinking of Padre Valencia," volunteered one. "Just as I was praying to him to not abandon us," another added.

And although the *Asilo* was far from town, the news spread immediately. Farmers passing by on their way to market took the amazing news with them. And people who would never have thought of visiting the *Asilo,* now could not be held back. *¡Un aura blanca!* No one had ever seen one before.

So they went to see the bird, for which the lepers had built a simple cage. And they were reminded of Padre Valencia, whose forgotten words of charity and compassion were reawakened in their minds. They were moved by the lepers, who hung back in order to allow people to admire the bird. And donations began to flow once more.

The *aura blanca* lived for several years. People wondered if it was simply an albino bird and argued why none had ever been seen before or after.

To the lepers, the bird offered inspiration and comfort. Those who had known Padre Valencia felt his presence among them and drew courage and strength from his memory. They knew that beyond their sick bodies, something bright and luminous would always exist. Those who had not previously known Padre Valencia now learned about him and, seeing their fellow sufferers inspired, were inspired as well.

When the *aura* died, it was embalmed and taken on tour throughout the island. Donations flowed to the lepers from wherever the *aura* went.

Years later, the government centralized the treatment of people with leprosy. The *Asilo San Lázaro* was renamed *Asilo Padre Valencia*, and turned over to the care of old people. Yet we still used the old name, names being hard to change in a traditional town like Camagüey. And Padre Valencia's cell remained intact. One could still see the narrow boards he had once used for a bed, the brick on which he had rested his tired head, and on a wooden perch, the embalmed body of the mysterious *aura blanca.* ❦

◆ ALMA FLOR ADA ◆

6 YEARS OLD

STORM!

Every morning, when I was a very young child, my grandmother would come silently into my room while I was still sleeping. I would wake up in her arms, fragrant with ylang-ylang, which she gathered from a large tree by the entrance of the house and then dried to put in all her drawers. She would help me dress and then take me by the hand to go see the cows and to drink a glass of fresh and foamy milk.

The best cow, the one with the creamiest and most abundant milk, was called Lolita, just like my grandmother. No one considered this disrespectful. It was common to give a cow its owner's name.

But when I was seven years old we moved to the city after my uncle's death, all the cows were sold. After living in the city for a few years, we returned to live in *La Quintica,* a very small house by the river, built by my father with his own hands. The big house was too large. Now that the family had dispersed we could not afford to keep it up on our own, so it was leased out to a trucking company. Then one of my mother's cousins who had a farm gave us a cow. The cow was allowed to roam freely in a pasture on the other side of the river. Once a day, a neighboring farmer milked her for us.

My mother named the cow Matilde, in honor of her cousin's wife. It was a black cow with white spots, and from the day she arrived we never lacked fresh milk. The milk was so rich, we saved the cream to make our own butter.

Every day, I placed the cream in the refrigerator. Once a week, I gathered it in a bowl and stirred it over and over again with a wooden spoon. As it grew harder, I placed ice cubes in the bowl and continued to stir. Then I washed the hardened cream several times with cold water. The first few times the water was milky, but I kept on washing until the water was completely clear and the cool butter was resting on the bottom of the bowl, ready to be sprinkled with salt and spread on the freshly baked bread the baker had just brought in.

One reason the cow Matilde gave us so much milk was that she was going to have a calf. And we could not agree on what the calf's name would be. Felipe, after my mother's cousin? Lolita, after my grandmother's favorite cow?

One night we woke up, startled by the sound of thunder. Lightning had struck close to the house, which shook as if hit by an explosion. My father said he thought he heard the cow Matilde mooing in distress.

None of us heard anything except the cracks of thunder and the drumming rain. But my father, always proud of his good hearing, put on his overcoat and walked out into the torrent falling from the sky. The fading light from his lantern signaled to us that he had gone toward the wooden bridge. With the heavy rain, the river would be too full to ford at the crossing. My mother and I stayed up waiting for him. She warmed some milk on the stove and put some water to boil to make fresh coffee. Very soon, its strong aroma filled the house.

I accepted a cup of warm milk with some drops of heavy coffee, and soon fell asleep on the couch. When the thunder woke me again, my mother was on the porch. I joined her just at the moment a gust of wind sent a sheet of rain against the house, soaking us. But my mother refused to go back in, searching in the darkness for some sign of my father.

All of a sudden, a flash of lightning outlined the shape of what looked to be a horrible monster. Although shorter than a man, it had a monstrous head that made me think of the Minotaur in one of my grandmother's books of mythology. I shook with fear.

My mother instead ran toward the shadowy figure that was approaching our porch. Not knowing very well what to do, I followed her. Right then, another flash of lightning illuminated the night. As though struck by the bolt, the monster seemed to split in two as my father took the newborn calf that he had been carrying on his shoulders and placed it on its wobbling legs. Matilde, who had followed my father and her calf through the storm, stood nearby.

"What about calling it *Temporal*?" my father asked as he shook out his jacket. My mother laughed. Unquestionably,

Temporal, the Spanish word for "tropical storm," was a perfect name. She continued to laugh as she tried to dry the rainwater from my father's face. They both went in the house.

I stayed outside, soaking wet, watching Matilde lick her newborn calf as though the rain, which had become softer and softer, were not enough to clean him. ❦

Epilogue

Life in a small town had a very special flavor. Time seemed to move very slowly, as each day repeated the previous one. Any experience outside the ordinary received an enormous amount of attention and became the focus of everyone's conversation for many days to come.

For a small child eager to understand life, our town provided a wealth of information just from observing how people behaved. It was surprising that among a relatively small number of people there could be so much diversity—each person constituting a world of her own, of his own.

Today, many years later, from a great distance in both time and space, I find that much of what I learned back then is still fresh in my memory and continues to inform my understanding of life and its mysteries.

May these stories help you see the richness all around you . . . and the richness within you.

✦ ON THE PORCH OF LA QUÍNTICA ✦

MY MOTHER AND MY GRANDFATHER MODESTO
IN THE FRONT CHAIRS

✦ MY GRANDFATHER ✦

MEDARDO LAFUENTE RUBIO

✦ ALL FOUR OF US ✦

MY FATHER, SISTER, ME, AND MY MOTHER